Boy Saints

for Little Ones

WRITTEN BY KIMBERLY FRIES

ILLUSTRATED BY SUE KOUMA JOHNSON

First Edition: February 2019

Cover by Sue Kouma Johnson

ISBN-13: 9781795593625

This book is dedicated to my son, Thomas James.
May these courageous saints always guide and inspire you.

And to my husband, who always reminds our family:
"Our goal is to become saints!"

My little children, reflect on these words:
the Christian's treasure is not on earth but in heaven.
- St. John Vianney

St. Thomas Aquinas

Thomas loved learning about God. He was quiet, but very smart. He wanted to devote his life to study, so he became a Dominican friar. He wrote many important books about God, the angels, and Catholic truths. He also wrote songs about the Eucharist. Although Thomas had written much about God, he said that all of his writings seemed "like straw" compared to the great love and majesty of God.

What does it take to become a saint? Will it.
— St. Thomas Aquinas

ST. IGNATIUS

When Ignatius was a boy, he dreamed of being a chivalrous knight. He could not wait to do lots of great deeds. However, while he was resting after being wounded in a battle, he read a book about the saints that changed his life. Then Ignatius wanted to be a great knight for Christ! He formed a group of priests, called the Society of Jesus, and wrote a book about how we can live for Jesus.

Go forth and set the world on fire.

— St. Ignatius

St. Ignatius is surrounded by the motto of the Society of Jesus. A. M. D. G. stands for "Ad majorem Dei gloriam," which means, "For the Greater Glory of God."

St. John Vianney

When John was young, he wanted to become a brave and faithful priest. Studying was difficult for him since he was not good at learning Latin. But, he always persevered. Once John became a priest, he would listen to 11 to 16 hours of confessions a day. Even though he had a lot of trouble sleeping at night, he gave all of his energy to the work of God.

It is a beautiful thought, my children, that we have a Sacrament which heals the wounds of our soul!

-   St. John Vianney

St. John Vianney is shown wearing his stole because he was known for hearing many confessions.

St. Gregory

Gregory grew up in a very wealthy and holy family. He was very smart and studied for many years. Gregory decided to become a monk and was later elected to be the pope. He gave great attention to how the Mass should be prayed and the wonderful music that is used to worship God. But, more than anything, he loved helping his people become closer to Christ. He called himself, "servant of the servants of God."

Remember God more often than you breathe.

- St. Gregory

St. Gregory is surrounded by music notes because he composed a special kind of holy music, called Gregorian chant.

St. Francis
of Assisi

Francis wanted to be a great knight, rich and popular. But a day after he left for battle, Francis had a dream where God told him that he was to return home. Francis decided to pray more. He slowly fell in love with God and lived a life of poverty and preaching. Francis started the Franciscan Order of friars. He received the stigmata, marks on his hands and side, like Jesus received by being crucified.

I have been all things unholy. If God can work through me, He can work through anyone. — St. Francis

The hands of St. Francis are up in reverence to God's creation and to show the stigmata.

St. Patrick

When Patrick was fourteen years old, he was captured by Irish pirates. At twenty years old, he escaped and went back home to Britain. Soon after he returned home, he had a dream of getting a letter from Ireland, which said that the people there wanted him to teach them about God. He decided to study to be a priest. Later, as a bishop, Patrick went to Ireland to tell thousands of people about God.

I am certain in my heart that all that I am,
I have received from God. - St. Patrick

The snakes are a symbol of the evils of paganism in Ireland, which St. Patrick drove out.

St. Pio

At the age of five, Pio gave his life to God. When he was young, he could see and talk to Jesus, Mary, and his guardian angel. Later, he became a Capuchin friar and a priest. Padre Pio loved the Mass, the Rosary, and praying for the souls in purgatory. He received the stigmata, the wounds of Jesus, on his hands, feet, and side. Padre Pio performed many miracles and could even appear in two places at the same time.

Prayer is the best weapon we have;
it is the key to God's heart. - St. Pio

Do you see the cross behind St. Pio? He prayed very much about how Jesus suffered on the cross.

ST. JOHN BOSCO

When John was very young, he had a dream about helping other boys become holy. Later, John became a priest. He was a teacher and like a father to the boys he helped. The boys had poor working conditions and they had little education. John loved the boys and taught them circus tricks and other fun games. But, most importantly, he taught them about Jesus.

Walk with your feet on earth,
but in your heart be in heaven.
- St. John Bosco

St. John Bosco always had a peaceful smile. The light-blue halo around his head represents holiness.

St. Augustine

Augustine was a smart boy, but he acted very badly and did not believe in God. After years of his mother's prayers for him, he became convinced that God does exist. Still, he feared that he was not worthy of God's love. After reading about many of the saints, Augustine learned about God's great mercy and love for him. Later, he became a writer, a priest, and even a bishop.

The greatest kindness one can render to any man is leading him to truth. – St. Augustine

The burning heart above St. Augustine represents his burning love for Christ.

SAINT JOHN

HENRY NEWMAN

John was a priest, writer, and great speaker. However, he was not Catholic until he was 44 years old, when he learned that the Catholic Church is the church that Jesus established. Later, he became a cardinal, an important position in the Church. His motto was, "*Cor ad cor loquitur*"—"Heart speaks to heart," since during prayer we speak to the heart of God, and God speaks back to our hearts.

The first duty of charity is to try and enter into the mind and feelings of others.— St. John Henry Neumann

Because Bl. John was a cardinal, he wore a red hat, a symbol of Christ's blood.

St. Maximilian

At 10 years old, Maximilian had a dream of Mary. She offered him a white crown, for purity, and a red crown, for martyrdom. Maximilian chose both because he wanted to be both pure and a martyr. He became a Franciscan and wanted to bring the whole world to Mary. During World War II, he was taken to a prison, where he offered his life so that another man could live.

Let us remember that love lives through sacrifice and is nourished by giving. - St. Maximilian

St. Maximilian was so devoted to Mary. He is holding an icon of the Polish Madonna.

St. George

George was a brave soldier and a Christian. One day, the head of the army announced that all Christians would be arrested and killed. George decided not to hide that he was a Christian. Before he died, George gave his money to the poor. He was then tortured and died a martyr, which means he died for his Catholic Faith.

St. George, Heroic Catholic soldier and defender of your Faith, obtain for us the great grace of heroic Christian courage that should mark soldiers of Christ. Amen

St. George is shown slaying the dragon, a symbol of the devil.

COLLECT ALL THE
MY LITTLE NAZARETH BOOKS

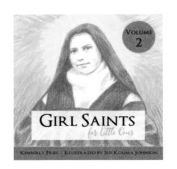
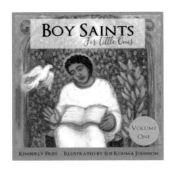

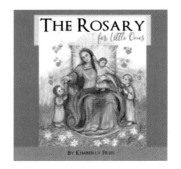
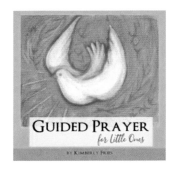

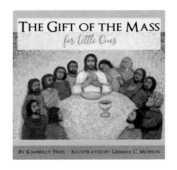

About the Author

Kimberly Fries lives in South Dakota with her husband and three young children. She has an Elementary Education degree and is a stay-at-home mom and blogger. She loves teaching her children about the Catholic Faith through beautiful books and is excited to write many more. Find her blog at www.mylittlenazareth.com.

About the Illustrator

Sue Kouma Johnson lives in Nebraska with her husband. After earning her BFA, she devoted her time to raising five children. Now she has taken up her calling as a Catholic artist, painting saints and images that express her love for her Catholic Faith.

See more of her artwork at www.catholicartandjewelry.com and visit her Etsy shop at www.etsy.com/shop/TreeOfHeaven.

Did you enjoy this book?
Please write a review at Amazon.com.
Spread the word about my books on social media.

Want to learn more about my books?
And be the first to know about my new releases?
Follow me on Facebook at
www.facebook.com/mylittlenazareth

Interested in getting twenty or more books at a wholesale price?
E-mail me at mylittlenazareth@gmail.com

Made in the USA
Las Vegas, NV
27 November 2020